Solas
Sólás

Christine Broe

Swan Press

Published by Swan Press
32 Joy Street
Dublin 4

Copyright © Christine Broe 2003

ISBN   0 9539205 2 6

Cover painting/design by author

Printed: Enprint, Churchtown, Dublin 14

For Tommy Nelson

'And we are put on earth a little space,
That we may learn to bear the beams of love.'

                      William Blake *Songs of Innocence*
                      'The Little Black Boy'

ACKNOWLEDGEMENTS

Acknowledgements are due to the following publications:
Extended Wings 2, 3, 4, Quintet, Women's Works 7, 8, 9, Acorn, Electric Acorn, Cuirt Journal, West 47, New Series Departures, Vol 3, RIPOSTE, InCognito, Asylum, The Green Dragon (Wales), *Books Ireland, Poetry Ireland, The Literary Review* (USA), *The Shop.*

Some of the poems in *Solas Sólás* were read on *Tonight with Vincent Browne,* RTE1.

Thanks to my *sisterpoetfriend,* Mary Shine, whose editorial skills gave shape to this book. Thanks also to all members, past and present of Rathmines, Syllables, and the Dublin Writers' Workshops, for your friendship, support and advice over many years.

CONTENTS

Solas

Riding White Horses	9
Before Light	10
Needing No Name	12
The White Door	13
At the Eleventh Hour	15
The Colour Orange	16
What Will Survive Of Us Is Love	18
Regaining Paradise	19
O	21
Famine Potatoes	22
The Tear Trees	23
Thursday 26th	24
No Poem	25
Poetic Phrases 5 for 50p	27

Dovetailed

Angel Art	31
Stolen Time	32
Remembering Kevin	33
Subversive	34
Of Human Kindness	35
Different Ways	36
Word for Windows	37

A Boy!	38
Terminal	39
Cribs	41
Naming the Sorrow	43
Coming Towards the End	44
Don't Bury Me . . .	45

Sólás

My Mother Brings Me Gifts	49
Legacy of Bubbles	50
The Ultimate Gift	51
Love is a Golden Sorrow	52
Holy Thursday	53
Big Al	54
Waiting for My Mother to Die	56
No Placenta for Dying	59
Lonely as a Cloud	60
Would a Mother Forget Her Children?	61
All That Remains	62
Silent Mother	63
A Decent Full Stop	64
The Last Laugh	66
Blue Sun, Dry Sea	67
Feeling at Home in Mount Jerome	68

Solas

Riding White Horses

There are days
I feel the need
to vaporise
be part of the cycle
of mists
of streams
of rivers flowing
over stones
old bones of ships
silted in the dark
deep green
be a drop unseen
be the blue of the ocean

then days
when I remember
having once believed
we were made
of stardust

and some residue
then rises
to surf the silvery mountains
ride white horses
to places light years away

Before Light

Once
in that time
before light existed
he existed
in loneliness
and loneliness existed in him

and knowing only loneliness
and darkness
he learned to love the darkness
thinking it other than himself.

And darkness wrapped him
and darkness kissed him
touched his dark lips
tingled him
like a Braille of stars.

And in that time before light existed
she existed
and she existed in longing
and longing made a dark cave in her
a dark echo in her
her longing was.

And not knowing
what she longed for
she stretched into eternal night

wishing
for something other than night
something other than longing.

A notion of stars caressed her
with dreams of light.

And so in that time before light existed
he existed and she existed
in loneliness
and in longing
and in dreams of light.

And it was only a matter of time.

Needing No Name

Three days
I have been in a void,
empty of words, existing
in shades of quietness
wrapped in blue.

Closing my eyes, I see
lemon windows float,
bright screen savers
stretching
on sapphire skies,
spacing day into dusk,
dusk into darkness.

A slight turn of my ankle
can keep the moon
balanced on my toe,
while I live as
a lowest common denominator,
breathing in, breathing out,
needing no name.

The White Door

I have entered the space beyond the white door
to be
here
is to be not
alone.

My breath becomes accustomed to the stillness.
My skin becomes accustomed to the light.

The strength of the silence lifts me
with the ease of gentle flight,

the flight of a snow white feather
in a land already white,

a land
oblivious to difference
between day
between night.

The blessing of sleep is superfluous.
I am filled with turquoise light.

From cell after cell of my spirit
my inhibitions seep

languid movement
movement lucid

choreographing
a golden trance

sway
swayed
by innate rhythms
fear no longer
dance
dance
dance

At The Eleventh Hour

Reluctantly, I speak to you of dreams
for we live in a time when peace is feared.

I saw people carrying lanterns of blue,
come slowly from the houses one by one
and the shadows of the dead followed, watching.

I saw others paint red petals on the drums
so the sounds came muffled like heartbeats
the dead remembered. They came to listen.

And listening and watching, the dead mingled,
for only the living keep divisions.

If only you had seen them when they danced,
gathering red drum beats into roses,
twirling round blue lanterns
as on other nights they flew round stars,
you would dream with me now. Even reluctantly.

I speak to you of dreams, for we live
where peace is feared.

*The Colour Orange**

A gestation of months in concrete,
dank amniotic cell of despair,
he existed in palpable blackness,
thick sticky darkness touched his skin.

Air stifling, hooded grey limbo,
his head bound in a filthy shroud,
he was walked to defecate daily,
in the bowels of Beirut re-interred.

One day of that long longing
his *'shuffling acolyte'* came
to the door, laid a bowl of fruit
by the light of a candle flame.

A brown bowl with some apricots,
one banana, some cherries and nuts
and oranges oranges oranges
miraculous as suns.

The smell of the fruit leaped into him
and he began to dance,
mesmerised by colour
in somnambulant rage he danced,
he danced every dance he knew
and dances unknown to him
and the walls the walls were singing
to the orange diamond within,
the orange the colour orange
intoxicated him with joy
and the walls of his sarcophagus
became blue sea blue sky.

Drunk with understanding unstateable,
filled with love sublime,
orange light of his solitary solstice
danced on the Jordan, danced on the Boyne.

*This poem was inspired by Brian Keenan's *An Evil Cradling,* Vintage, 1993

'What will survive of us is love'*
(For Gordon Wilson)

What can I give you but the whiteness of my washing,
clean, limp and hanging,
so wind and sun will dry away its tears.
Take my bursting love at the feel
of a child's hair brushing my cheek,
asleep, a weight of love on my lap.

From this and every home you pass
soak up our love,
till you can no longer carry any more,
burdened with the surplus you have shared
since her hand reached out to you,
before the dust had settled.

Philip Larkin, *The Whitsun Weddings*, 'An Arundel Tomb',
Faber & Faber, 1964

Regaining Paradise

*. . . and when tomorrow had come
and he knew it was the day,
he opened his briefcase
and took out the trees.*

In the centre of moss green,
he placed them in a circle
around him, and sat.

Birch and beech, rowan and ash,
grew round him slowly breathing.
Holly and yew,
oak and elm,
willow and elder,
closed him in their circle.
Sylvan spirits circling slow
bathed him in emerald light,
dappled him in the thought free thoughts
of their green shade.

At his feet
an apple tree began
and grew so fast
with leaves of whitest green
and snowy rose bright blossoms
and one apple of the deepest red
he held
cold and waxy round
in his hands –
the beginning.

*. . . and his oak desk
sprouted leaves and acorns
to remember
how in his exile
he had touched wood.*

O

Be the sea that carries me,
be moon, be tides, be waves,
be lappings, be the sand.

Touch the body that I'm in,
rest your hand like golden
thoughts upon my hair. Be there

to taste the salty crystals
drying on my lips. Hold me.
Inhale my whispered sighs.
Lie with me

so I can hear the silence
that resonates in you.

Famine Potatoes

Cover us with earth
but remember
it is from our eyes
the translucent probes will grow,
reaching out into the dark

and on our subterranean arms
will grow new tubers,

some you'll eat
and some you'll sow for seed

and they will reach out
and multiply, multiply.

Remember
these are our eyes
that send the green shoots up,
like leafy periscopes searching suns
to violet tint our white bells
with their little pollen peals.

Still we silently mourn,
silently love the dead.

The Tear Trees
'It's surface tension that keeps them hanging on.'

Suspended rain drops shiver
on every silver birch tree,
science explains these things,
molecules we can't see, but

each tenacious little drop
carries windows of the sky,
each a single watery world,
countless millions we pass by.

A miracle of rain drops
hung to dry in a gentle breeze,
shivering wet they shine on us
from tree after silver tree.

We distract ourselves with beauty,
suspend grief, suspend fears,
and we never even mention
our own reservoir of tears.

Thursday 26 June 1997

There has been no summer.
Tourists stand wet under umbrellas,
or fortified by black Guinness,
face the musty dry passages
of Kilmainham Gaol, dripping.
Yesterday I cried all day.

This morning the wipers reveal only
the shadow of dull chestnuts
on long lines of traffic.
I hear the *AA Roadwatch* say
that Harold's Cross is heavy.
This grey June is pressing on my head.

At Seapoint the sodden blue flag
is wrapped around the pole.
A sole bather trudges over ridged grey sand,
plodding through the rain in search of water.
The tide is out.

No Poem

The pencil squiggles –
let it twist,
the line of words that come
come only from the wrist.

Eight bones –
the westerly most
resting on the page
as I face the window.

White space –
if I were a snail
my silvery afterthoughts
at least would leave a trail
to shine
in the absence of a poem.

White page –
product of some tree
sacrificed, bleached,
set out upon a table
for pulp fiction.

In a state of too much mind
where do I find

white space

where words will settle,
where feeling and image will copulate.
cause a silent echo
in their wake.

I am not the vessel for such gift
today.

I put the full stop here

Poetic phrases 5 for 50p
oblique classical reference Free!

After I cut the poem to the bone,
was left with amputated clauses
and orphaned phrases,
whole verses balled up
and flung into corners,
Paddy McElroy* came to mind.

He was the man for salvage,
precious was the metal word,
every filing was saved
every sliver of silver.

On asbestos mats
we piled our little hoards
and like dragons linked
to ancient Bunsen burners,
we breathed flames of blue
on silver rivers flowing
backwards into spheres.
Molten mercury.

I've never since felt
closer to the gods.

*Paddy McElroy taught at NCAD in the 1960s

Dovetailed

Angel Art

What angel took the picture
the day you washed the cabbage
in the sun,
that after all these years
the image burns my inner eye.
Chin high at your yellow sink
I watched you hold each cup-shaped leaf
beneath the cleansing flow.
A green green drowned forest,
you kept submerged
till little bubble diamonds hatched,
then shaking leaves –
me accidentally blessed.

Stolen Times

The first present he gave her -
it's gold links held her wrist
for many years.

Even after he died
its gold hands circled her days.
The pulses first a metronome of loss,
then timing moments of not remembering,
whole minutes of forgetfulness,
happier hours when grandchildren
he had never known
were tick tocked into naps.

Then
some robber came
and snatched it for a fix.

Her naked wrist is handcuffed to the loss.

Remembering Kevin

The smell of him lingered
around silver papers
he'd collected for the blind,
in a miniature sideboard
made when he learned dovetail joints.

In his lonely room
the golden flakes of woodbine
drifting into cobwebbed corners,
were no antidote to the whiff
of single socks, long lost
under an unmade bed.

The black tie,
that helped choke back
his graveside tears,
lay still knotted on the chair, as

little by little
he cleared the house
of her treasures
to buy black solace,
sipped in Fallon's snug.

Subversive

'Don't open that door,' they told her.
'You can trust no one these days'.

She watches at the window,
can see them waiting on the roofs.
She stashes away food,
bread, in her cardigan pockets.

She knows the time of their comings and goings,
so when her minders have left 'the buildings'
before they reach *Blackpits,*
she moves slowly, painfully, to the door.

Instantly they *whoosh* down,
leave no scrap of evidence around her feet.
Later as she watches *Fair City* on the telly,
they swoop over her house in a twenty one dove salute.

... *Of Human Kindness*

Just as I finished the ceiling, he looked in.
'There's no milk,' he said.

An instant flash feasibility study
persuaded me,
of the improbability
of a middle aged,
post-lactating female
successfully breast-feeding
a pot-bellied menopausal male,
from the top rung of a stepladder.

Wickedly,
in delicious slow motion,
I could see half a tin
of brilliant white matt emulsion,
(a bargain from Coughlan's in Meath Street),
sail splashing through the knife-cut silence.
Couch potato 'au lait!'
ole! ole! ole!

'There's money on the mantlepiece,
but don't make tea for me,' I said,

'I'm going for a pint!'

Different Ways

That last day on the mountain
the wind had changed, still
you took the difficult descent
abseiling down black pistes
into the snow bowl.

I took my time on blue slopes
gliding through pines
living every curve
of that last white adultery
with the mountain.

Word For Windows

At three a.m. she rang me from the station,
the long anticipated echo
of the ringing in my ears.

I answered in the dark,
then flinging back the shutters
the moon threw a window on the wall.
A window in the mirror made
a window on the ceiling, white
light falling down through moonbeams
opened windows on the floor.

Micro   softword   Aoife.

A boy!

No weary wise men
trailed east to Holles Street
the night that you were born.

No smelly camels
were tethered to the railings.

No telltale whiff of frankincense
lingered in the lifts.

No dusting of gold sand
puzzled the cleaners on the early shift.

There was no alleluia chorus.

But pigeons came from Ringsend
to coo on the window sills
and the morning light lay gently on me
and lit the orchids tied in blue.

I lifted you again
getting used to the weight of the gift
of another child born
under a coincidence of stars.

Terminal
(For Sarah)

Crossing the sleeping city,
gull cries anticipate the dawn.

The lights are against us.
At Adam and Eve's we stop.

A Holles Street feeling washes over me.
The first hungry grippings at my breast.

So many of our journeys start
at this lemon hour of light.

Unfinished cups of tea
still on the table,
abandoned,
as we sat on cases,
strained the zips to contain
the last of your after thoughts.

You are silent beside me,
preoccupied.

You answer me in German when I speak
already tuned to the frequency of your arrival.
'Agus leat féin'* I say, getting my own back
and 'go n'éirigh an *flughasen* leat'.*

At the departure gates you wave,
blow kisses on your fingers
and shine them on the collar
of your brother's leather jacket,
I notice only then you've nicked.
We part laughing

and all the way home
I fool myself, thinking finally
I delivered you without pain.

*agus leat féin: and with you also
*go n'éirigh an flughasen leat: may the airport rise with you

Cribs

Mother of God
did your postnatal regime involve
kneeling, robed in blue,
hands joined,
head inclined slightly to the left?

I cannot believe it.

Mother of God
did you really leave your infant
lying stretched in the straw,
surrounded by this plaster cast of men?

I cannot believe it.

Mother of God
with shepherds, kings and angels
descending from all sides,
did you not hold your baby to your breast
and pray for your sisters?

What can I believe?

. . . when Joseph had cut the cord
and she lay back in the straw
to rest her sweat-soaked head on his cloak,
he cleaned the baby
as best he could in the circumstances

and laid him in her arms.
His tiny fist closed around her finger,
as she suckled him
saying 'This is his body'.

. . . and it came to pass that she slept a while
and while she slept two women came
one carrying some bread
and one a pitcher of water
or maybe wine.

This I can believe.

Naming The Sorrow

Long years I wished for you, wanted you, willed you,
and every moon month raged and wept
when disappointment flowed.

And then at last your golden beat
was pulsing in my darkness,
making me so secret and whole.

Twelve weeks,
a white fish
with big black eyes,
I held you,
baptising you in a river of tears
till they took you away.

I called, called, would have called you Alice.

Coming Towards The End

At the open door
we speak, say at last
what had been left
unsaid.

The light
throws our shadows
into the garden.

I journey home
carrying the rose.

Just before sleep,
a sudden surrounding
of salmon light.
I feel you near

and try to send my body
to travel with you
in a dream,

to let it happen
with no thought,

but effort makes
the colour fade.

At dawn
your rose
a cold black shadow
against the coming day.

Don't bury me in anything
I wouldn't be seen dead in

Shroud me in satin,
white mist, clouds
air brushed, violet
evenings, hyacinth
blue of bells blending
moss softened greens
and yellow,
bright yellow roses
in sunset's warm orange.
And gather me amber
and rubies and garnets red
to garland my black birth,
when darkness swathes me
in every colour known
and I slip into colours
never even dreamed of.

Sólás

Dedicated to the memory of my mother,
Pauline Broe, who died of Alzheimer's disease
on the 21 April 2001

My Mother Brings Me Gifts

Day by day
she gives me
snatches of conversations
held in waves
of sound forever,
the words remembered,

and day by day
she dredges up the jokes
passed on
with years of telling,
the script secure – she's happy
when I laugh –

and everyday
presents me,
from the drift of all forgotten,
with pictures of her father
lighting candle after candle,
and her mother pouring water
from a glass carafe.

She leaves me
day by day
these gifts,
precious salvage
of a life lost
in a sea of forgetfulness.

A Legacy of Bubbles

Palmolive scented ghosts
waft by my windowsill

wisps of she
who passed to me
this fragile skill.

With delicate breath
I whisper into being
rainbow-windowed worlds

cup-shaped bubbles
distend
a moment
cling to me.

Here
in iridescent sphere
I caress impermanence

and bubble
after bubble
holds a legacy of love
I cannot wash my hands of.

The Ultimate Gift

Carefully she carried it
 across the room
a silver spoon of water

and carefully
I took it from her
not spilling a drop.

'Thank you,' I said,
and raised it slowly
to my lips.

Love Is A Golden Sorrow

Where will I weep for you
now that the willow is gone,
lying with leafless branches
through the rushes and reeds,
trailing blond hair through water
in the February night,
oblivious of spring?

There must have been a scream
on that silent, windless night,
a tearing of roots
that no one heard,
and stars dimmed one by one
and the sun rose, unobscured
by the willow's silhouette
against the dawn.

I weep for the willow
by this ruptured patch of earth,
at each sapling staked
along the water's edge.
A deep river flows forever
where once the willow wept
but where will I weep for you?

Holy Thursday

Not for the liturgical significance
or any high or holy motive
but for shame, I washed her feet.

For the sake of the chiropodist's
olfactory senses as he studied the corn,
I washed her feet.

The corn for which, had they an inkling
of its powers, the meteorological office
would have bartered eye teeth.

The corn under whose pressure
she has become
geriatric actress of the year. Jesus.

I washed her feet, and I prayed
that this woman would be taken from me.

Big Al

It's all because of Al
she's for the birds - tweet tweet -
sitting on the jacks at four a.m.
with rubber gloves on her feet.

When I locked up the rice crispies
she went snap crackle and pop . . .
and shredded the budgie's millet spray
into a bowl of slop . . .

Since she's started this affair with Al
she collects the oddest things.
Spoons, bananas, and toilet rolls
in our house have sprouted wings.

Tayto crisps, lego men,
heads of celery, I swear,
disappear before our eyes
as if they were never there.

This magpie syndrome's caused by Al.
I know I shouldn't slag
but everything that's missing
turns up in her bag.

Eileen says her Ma's the same
but that woman's got more class,
under Al's strange power, she
nicks Waterford crystal glass.

My Mam's having an affair with Al,
once there was no woman finer
now she's for the birds
and I blame him, you know your man,
Al Zheimer.

Waiting For My Mother To Die

I lived in fear of the gods
of imperceptible change.
When people asked, I said
'she's just the same.'
They never knew
that every day I prayed
to the angel of death.

I envied them their funerals.
The neatly packaged end.
The flowers, the candles, sympathy,
the plot.

In fantasy I saw men in black
slink up the side aisles
like sewer rats on castors,
yellow faces through the incense haze.

Day after day
the nightmare was the same
and then one day it fused into a dream,
and from the holy altar angels came
marvellous and unmarbled,
and winged her above their heads
and dressed in white we followed
leaving trails of funeral flowers.
We danced to the door
people opening
as a wave before

and flowing behind us
down Thomas' Road
through snow storms
of cherry blossoms.
Neighbours waved
remembering her
lighter and lighter
till she became the dance.

Mother
down streets the very cobbles
remembering you
the stones singing out
remembering you
the people we pass
remembered you
the people past
remembering you
lighter past New Market
New Row lighter till
it seemed we carried a dream
a dream remembering a people
remembering a dream
dancing a dream
we carried you
cloud mother
dancing
remembering you
and the more we danced
the more you disappeared
till nothing was left
at Dean Street
but us dancing.

. . . and so letting go
I can love you again.
Be beside you.
Watch you
preoccupied with roses
place each leg of the Zimmer frame
in the centre of a flower, pink
slow progress down dove grey corridors
to the garden
where sometimes I sing to you
and sometimes
you even seem to know me.

No Placenta For Dying

And if
*'the past grows gradually around one
like a placenta for dying'**
even that's denied her,
trapped in a perpetual present
in a time shrunken to the moment.

Again and again for the first time
she folds the towel,
carries the towel from chair
to identical chair, from room
to identical room,
the womb of her past denied her.

Again and again
she lifts the cup,
circles the rim with her finger,
peering into the emptiness.

Helpless as our images
framed on her locker,
we watch
and there's no way to deliver her
from this aborted death.

*John Berger, *And Our Faces, My Heart, Brief As Photos,* Vintage, 1992

'... lonely as a cloud'

'Yellow,' she says,
stroking her mohair jacket,
single strands of indigo,
lilac and Prussian blue,
catching the evening light.

'Yellow,' she says,
fingering the blue blue buttons,
'not in so much as it's . . .
daffodils . . . but it feels . . .
comfortable . . . as such . . .'

And it makes as much sense
as anything . . . now
she wanders . . .

'Yellow,' she said,
snuggling into
her fluffy jacket,
strands of indigo,
lilac and deep blue,
forever holding light.

'Yellow,' she said,
touching . . . sky blue
   . . . daffodils.

Would A Mother Forget Her Children?

A part of me is dead, can feel no pain,
the part that feared, has nothing left to fear,
now you who gave me birth forget my name.

A stranger now, my visits you disdain.
I come, I see you, and I leave you here
and part of me is dead, can feel no pain.

I try to jog your memory in vain,
hand you photographs of those you once held dear,
but you who gave us birth forget our names.

Demolished, derelict your memory lane,
we miss your wicked wit, your Dublin sneer.
Part of us is dead and can feel no pain.

Just a shell of a woman, you became
empty of us, oblivious of years,
you gave us birth and now forget our names.

Nameless we come, while breath in you remains.
We'll not forget you, though bereft of tears.
A part of us is dead, can feel no pain
now you who gave us birth forget our names.

All That Remains

It takes at least two of me to go and see my mother,
then vacantly she looks at me as if we are not there,
but we walk with her, this me she does not see,
and the me that's watching me, silently all three. We walk.

Like marathon monks we wander eternally past doors.
If we try to rest and hold her hands, she stands
and leads us by that locked door to the last room

where, residing side by side, are shells of women, curved
brittle, translucent, light, cared for by nurses in white,
who lay them in soft places, so sun can shine on empty faces.

Part of me wants to believe this is a tabernacle here,
the other part no longer believes and is bereft of tears.

Silent Mother

Your world is shrinking,
your body shrivelled,
you hold my hand.

I long for words,
words you'll never say,
words that hold the power
of unutterable thoughts
lodged in the tissue,
in the cells.

You leave me a legacy of secrets.
I will scatter them
with every last word I can gather.
Shatter this silence profound.

A Decent Full Stop

There are enough words in the world,
more than enough,
when all that is necessary
communicates itself in silence.

Should the sparkle of a sapphire speak
or be some window in your eye
that tells of love?

The script is done.
You have said all you will say.
I listen to the pregnant silence
for sudden intakes of breath.
Sighs.

Silent Mother
I am learning
to live with the absence

with a language beyond
even that between the lines.

We walk together,
I synchronise my steps to yours,
from garden gate to garden gate
sealed with cobwebs.
You touch the locks.

Scents of flowers caress us,
sitting in the sun,
when your hand unbidden reaches out,
catches mine
and we are joined to everything.

The Last Laugh

*When I prayed for the death of a loved one
did I forfeit the blessing of tears?*

Numb.
I live in a body of dehydrated tears.
A salt cave, I echo hollow of all,
of all.

Could tears wash away the silent years,
tears drown the soundless thief, who
wiped her voice, who
swallowed her songs, who
left me arid grief?

I am made of the salt of an ocean,
of an ocean and a half.
I would weep the lot
if once more I could hear
the sound of her full-hearted laugh.

Blue Sun, Dry Sea

Doused of its golden light
blue sun
sun
blue iris of eternity

Shards of sapphire
cut the light
birthed death
unbirthed life

Only sound
huge hollow sound
from the souls of all the creatures
I'd forgotten how to be
howled in me

Dark sound
deep dwelling sound
dwelt in the desert
that dwelt in me

I knelt in me

Dry sobs shuddered through me,
shook me, caved me
to the bed of the bone dry sea

I clawed for a well of tears
a tide of blessing tears
to wash me
wash me

Feeling At Home In Mount Jerome

Inside the old church
another curtain closes,
piped music drifts across
parked cars,
to the café next door.

Your man behind the counter
doesn't bat an eyelid,
the quintessential Dubliner -
he's seen it all before.
There are mugs for tea or coffee,
chocolate bars in boxes,
cakes under plastic lids.

Old habits never leave us,
we all agree, choose different cakes,
then break them,
swap and share them, saying:
'It wasn't off the stones we licked this.'
Sisters round the table laughing,
a year to the day.